# 20<sup>TH</sup> CENTURY ART

## 1980-2000

## NEW MEDIA, NEW MESSAGES

Please visit our web site at: www.garethstevens.com
For a free color catalog describing Gareth Stevens' list of high-quality books
and multimedia programs, call 1-800-542-2595 (USA) or 1-800-461-9120 (Canada).
Gareth Stevens Publishing's Fax: (414) 332-3567.

Library of Congress Cataloging-in-Publication Data available upon request from publisher.
Fax (414) 336-0157 for the attention of the Publishing Records Department.

ISBN 0-8368-2853-4

This North American edition first published in 2001 by
**Gareth Stevens Publishing**
A World Almanac Education Group Company
330 West Olive Street, Suite 100
Milwaukee, WI 53212 USA

Original edition © 2000 by David West Children's Books. First published in Great Britain in 2000 by
Heinemann Library, Halley Court, Jordan Hill, Oxford OX2 8EJ, a division of Reed Educational and
Professional Publishing Limited. This U.S. edition © 2001 by Gareth Stevens, Inc. Additional end
matter © 2001 by Gareth Stevens, Inc.

Picture Research: Brooks Krikler Research
Picture Editor: Carlotta Cooper
Gareth Stevens Editor: Dorothy L. Gibbs

Photo Credits:
Abbreviations: (t) top, (m) middle, (b) bottom, (l) left, (r) right

AKG London: pages 4-5(b), 26(t), 27(l).
Bridgeman Art Library: page 24(t).
Bridgeman Art Library © ADAGP, Paris, and DACS, London, 2000: page 16.
Bridgeman Art Library Private Collection: page 23(t).
Corbis: pages 13(b), 14(b), 15(b), 17(tl, tr), 22(t).
Corbis © ARS, New York, and DACS, London, 2000: page 6(r).
Paul Nightingale: page 8(bl).
Rex Features: pages 3, 6(l), 8(bm), 9(b), 10(both), 11(b), 12(t), 13, 18(b), 19(t), 20(both), 21(b),
    22(b), 25(t), 26(b), 27(r).
The Saatchi Gallery, London: pages 7, 21(t).
Frank Spooner Pictures: pages 4-5(t), 5(both), 8-9, 9(t), 12(b), 14(t), 23(b), 24(b), 28, 29(b).
Tate Gallery Archive: page 15(m).
Tate Gallery © Anselm Kiefer: cover, page 13(t).
Tate Gallery © DACS 2000: pages 18(t), 25(b).
Tate Gallery © Gerhard Richter: page 11(t).
Tate Gallery © Julian Schnabel: page 15(t).
Tate Gallery © VAGA, New York, and DACS, London, 2000: page 19(b).

Printed in the United States of America

1 2 3 4 5 6 7 8 9 05 04 03 02 01

# 20<sup>TH</sup> CENTURY ART

# 1980-2000

## NEW MEDIA, NEW MESSAGES

## Clare Oliver

**Gareth Stevens Publishing**

A WORLD ALMANAC EDUCATION GROUP COMPANY

# CONTENTS

*The 1980s and 1990s saw the decline of Communism. With the fall of the Wall in 1989, Berlin became a single city again. The Soviet Union officially broke apart in 1991.*

*Nam June Paik is credited with creating, in 1965, the first piece of video art. He continued to make his multimonitor video displays on into the 1990s.*

HIGH TECH ALLERGY (DETAIL),
*Nam June Paik, 1995*

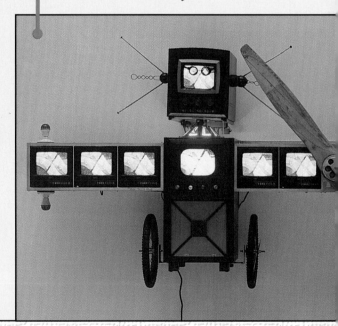

# NEW STYLES AND STARS

In the last two decades of the 20th century, new media for art, including photography, video, and computers, gained acceptance. The computer revolution hit full force after the mid 1980s, when the Internet was opened to public access.

Old art forms, however, were not dead. Sculpture was well-supported. The financial boom of the 1980s meant more commissions for sculptors. Painting, which had been largely neglected during the 1960s and 1970s, reappeared. In the United States, new movements, such as neo-Expressionism and Graffiti Art, gave rise to the brightest art stars since Andy Warhol. Big names included Julian Schnabel, Jean-Michel Basquiat, and Kitsch artist Jeff Koons. In the 1990s, the focus shifted to London as Damien Hirst shocked the world with his displays of pickled animals. By the dawn of the 21st century, the boundaries of art had been pushed further than ever before.

Toy Story *made motion picture history in 1995 as the first full-length feature film produced entirely by computer. Only short bursts of computer-generated special effects were used in earlier movies.*

5

*As technology took huge leaps forward, Bill Gates, the founder of Microsoft, made millions.*

# WORLDS OF WORDS

Since the 1960s, conceptual artists have used words in their art as a way to convey the idea or "meaning" of a work.

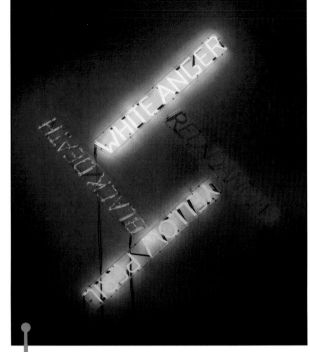

WHITE ANGER/RED DANGER/
YELLOW PERIL/BLACK DEATH,
*Bruce Nauman, 1985*

*This neon sculpture exposes deep-rooted racism. The words paired with red, white, and black seem to be normal, obvious word associations, but combining "yellow" with "peril" forms an unpleasant nickname used, in the past, to refer to the Chinese.*

## WORD ASSOCIATION

American artist Bruce Nauman (*b.* 1941) has worked in different media, including performance art and Video Art, for four decades, yet he is best known for his neon word sculptures. Their thought-provoking words seem to sum up the nature of existence. Phrases in his *One Hundred Live and Die* (1984) include "Rage and Die" and "Think and Live." The phrases often read like the word association tests used to help diagnose mental illness. These tests tap into a patient's subconsious, or inner mind, by asking the person to look at a word or a picture and say the first word or phrase that comes to mind.

*Songwriter Kurt Cobain (1967–1994) was the scruffy lead singer for the popular grunge band Nirvana.*

### GENERATION GRUNGE

In his book *Generation X*, Douglas Coupland identified the "slacker" generation. Coupland argued that, in the 1990s, with nothing left to fight for, anxiety-ridden young people were adopting a directionless lifestyle. This lack of direction was evident in grunge music, which was often about being bored.

## ALL IN THE MIND

New York artist Sean Landers (*b.* 1962) also employs words that seem to pour from the subconscious. Using a very small brush, he fills a canvas with poems or strings of tiny words. "See I wanted to paint pictures," he explains, "but I wasn't that great at it so I decided to write on them to make them better. And check it out, it worked!"

6

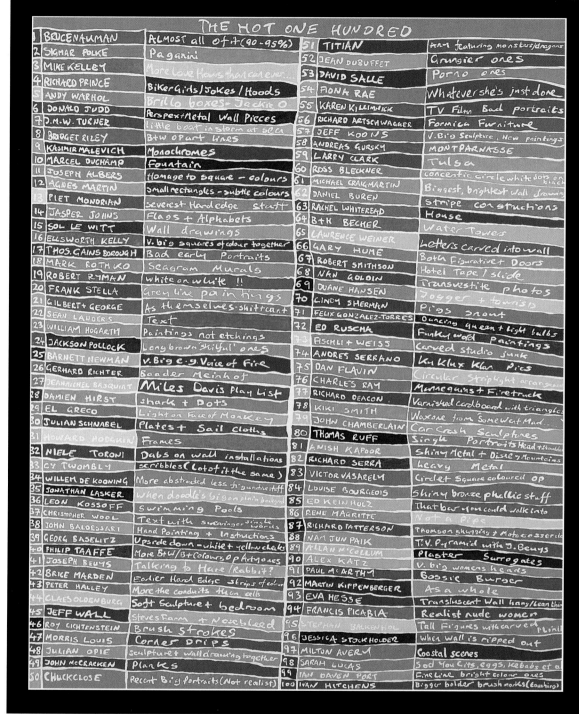

## THE HOT ONE HUNDRED

| # | Artist | Work | # | Artist | Work |
|---|--------|------|---|--------|------|
| 1 | BRUCE NAUMAN | ALMOST all of it (90-95%) | 51 | TITIAN | Any featuring monsters/dragons |
| 2 | SIGMAR POLKE | Paganini | 52 | JEAN DUBUFFET | Grungier ones |
| 3 | MIKE KELLEY | More Love Hours than can ever… | 53 | DAVID SALLE | Porno ones |
| 4 | RICHARD PRINCE | Biker Girls/Jokes/Hoods | 54 | FIONA RAE | Whatever she's just done |
| 5 | ANDY WARHOL | Brillo boxes - Jackie O | 55 | KAREN KILLIMNICK | TV Film Bad portraits |
| 6 | DONALD JUDD | Perspex + Metal Wall Pieces | 56 | RICHARD ARTSCHWAGGER | Formica Furniture |
| 7 | J.M.W. TURNER | little boat in storm at sea | 57 | JEFF KOONS | V. Big Sculpture, New paintings |
| 8 | BRIDGET RILEY | B+W Op art lines | 58 | ANDREAS GURSKY | MONTPARNASSE |
| 9 | KASIMIR MALEVICH | Monochromes | 59 | LARRY CLARK | Tulsa |
| 10 | MARCEL DUCHAMP | Fountain | 60 | ROSS BLECKNER | concentric circle white dots on black |
| 11 | JOSEPH ALBERS | Homage to square - colours | 61 | MICHAEL CRAIG-MARTIN | Biggest, brightest wall drawn |
| 12 | AGNES MARTIN | Small rectangles - subtle colours | 62 | DANIEL BUREN | stripe constructions |
| 13 | PIET MONDRIAN | severest Hard edge stuff | 63 | RACHEL WHITEREAD | House |
| 14 | JASPER JOHNS | Flags + Alphabets | 64 | B+H BECKER | Water Towers |
| 15 | SOL LE WITT | Wall drawings | 65 | LAWRENCE WEINER | Letters carved into wall |
| 16 | ELLSWORTH KELLY | V. big squares of colour together | 66 | GARY HUME | Both Figurative + Doors |
| 17 | THOS. GAINSBOROUGH | Bad early Portraits | 67 | ROBERT SMITHSON | Hotel Tape / slide |
| 18 | MARK ROTHKO | Seagram Murals | 68 | NAN GOLDIN | Transvestite photos |
| 19 | ROBERT RYMAN | white on white !! | 69 | DUANE HANSEN | Jogger + tourists |
| 20 | FRANK STELLA | Grey line paintings | 70 | CINDY SHERMAN | Pigs snout |
| 21 | GILBERT + GEORGE | As themselves - shit cunt | 71 | FELIX GONZALEZ-TORRES | Dancing queen + light bulbs |
| 22 | SEAN LANDERS | Text | 72 | ED RUSCHA | Funky word Paintings |
| 23 | WILLIAM HOGARTH | Paintings not etchings | 73 | FISCHLI + WEISS | Carved studio junk |
| 24 | JACKSON POLLOCK | Long brown 'skilful' ones | 74 | ANDRES SERRANO | Ku Klux Klan Pics |
| 25 | BARNETT NEWMAN | V. Big e.g. Voice of Fire | 75 | DAN FLAVIN | Circular Striplight arrangement |
| 26 | GERHARD RICHTER | Baader Meinhof | 76 | CHARLES RAY | Mannequins + Firetruck |
| 27 | JEAN-MICHEL BASQUIAT | Miles Davis Play List | 77 | RICHARD DEACON | Varnished cardboard with triangles |
| 28 | DAMIEN HIRST | shark + Dots | 78 | KIKI SMITH | Waxone from 'Somewhat Mad… |
| 29 | EL GRECO | Light on Face of Monkey | 79 | JOHN CHAMBERLAIN | Car Crash Sculptures |
| 30 | JULIAN SCHNABEL | Plates + Sail cloths | 80 | THOMAS RUFF | Single Portraits Head + shoulders |
| 31 | HOWARD HODGKIN | Frames | 81 | ANISH KAPOOR | Shiny Metal + Disney Mountains |
| 32 | NIELE TORONI | Dabs on wall installations | 82 | RICHARD SERRA | heavy Metal |
| 33 | CY TWOMBLY | scribbles (Lot of it the same) | 83 | VICTOR VASARELY | Circle + Square coloured OP |
| 34 | WILLEM DE KOONING | More abstracted less figurative stuff | 84 | LOUISE BOURGEOIS | Shiny bronze phallic stuff |
| 35 | JONATHAN LASKER | When doodle's big on plain background | 85 | ED KEINHOLZ | That bar you could walk into |
| 36 | LEON KOSSOFF | Swimming Pools | 86 | RENE MAGRITTE | Not a Pipe |
| 37 | CHRISTOPHER WOOL | Text with swearing or single words | 87 | RICHARD PATTERSON | Thomson shagging + Motocross exercise |
| 38 | JOHN BALDESSARI | Hand Pointing + Instructions | 88 | NAM JUN PAIK | T.V. Pyramid with J. Beuys |
| 39 | GEORG BASELITZ | Upside down - white + yellow cheeks | 89 | ALLAN McCOLLUM | Plaster Surrogates |
| 40 | PHILIP TAAFFE | More B+W/B+Colours Op Art ones | 90 | ALEX KATZ | V. big womens heads |
| 41 | JOSEPH BEUYS | Talking to Hare/Rabbit? | 91 | PAUL McCARTHY | Bossie Burger |
| 42 | BRICE MARDEN | Earlier Hard Edge strips of colour | 92 | MARTIN KIPPENBERGER | As a whole |
| 43 | PETER HALLEY | More the conduits than cells | 93 | EVA HESSE | Transluscent Wall hang/lean thing |
| 44 | CLAES OLDENBURG | Soft Sculpture + bedroom | 94 | FRANCIS PICABIA | Realist nude women |
| 45 | JEFF WALL | Steves Farm + Nosebleed | 95 | STEPHAN BALKENHOL | Tall Figures with carved Plinth |
| 46 | ROY LICHTENSTEIN | Brush Strokes | 96 | JESSICA STOCKHOLDER | When Wall is ripped out |
| 47 | MORRIS LOUIS | Corner Drips | 97 | MILTON AVERY | Coastal scenes |
| 48 | JULIAN OPIE | sculpture + wall drawing together | 98 | SARAH LUCAS | Sod You Cats, eggs, kebabs et al |
| 49 | JOHN McCRACKEN | Planks | 99 | IAN DAVENPORT | Fine Line bright colour ones |
| 50 | CHUCK CLOSE | Recent Big portraits (Not realist) | 100 | IVAN HITCHENS | Bigger bolder brushmarks (touching) |

**THE HOT ONE HUNDRED**
PETER DAVIES, 1997

Peter Davies is known for his "artist league tables." On each list, the artists change positions. Bruce Nauman, for example, was at No. 1 on *The Hot One Hundred*. On *The Hip One Hundred* (1998), he had dropped to No. 9. Davies said his opinions change even while he is making a painting, so, by the time the painting is finished, he already disagrees with the order. Davies's lists show how short-lived celebrity can be, as well as how ideas change and evolve over time. The lists also show how fashion influences the way people look at art.

7

## SLACKER SEAN

Landers has come to stand for the slacker generation — the youth of the 1990s known for their despairing lack of ambition. The words in his pieces are often spelled wrong, and the ideas sometimes seem childish. Still, Sean Landers is a big success.

## IN AT NO. 1

In *Text-Painting* by Peter Davies (*b.* 1970), which lists the artists Davies liked, Landers is at No. 1. In response, Landers painted "Hey English guy whose copying my work and nameing me as the greatest artist. Thanks and youre right but youre eating into my profits."

# EXPLORING EMPTINESS

In the 1990s, Rachel Whiteread (*b.* 1963) became famous for her casts of negative spaces, such as the area under a bed. Minimalist sculptures, such as Whiteread's, are simple forms that allow the artist to explore concepts of time, space, and sound. One of the effects of these forms is a sense of emptiness.

### INSIDE OUT

Minimalist sculpture was not completely new in the 1990s. Bruce Nauman made a cast of the space under his chair in the 1960s. In 1993, however, Whiteread won the Turner Prize for *House*, a cast of the interior of an entire house that was going to be demolished. Whiteread cast the inside of a destroyed library for Vienna's Holocaust Memorial. In *Untitled (Book Corridors)* (1998), the concave spines of thousands of books commemorate the 65,000 Austrian Jews who died in the Holocaust during World War II.

## AT THE EDGE OF THE WORLD II
### ANISH KAPOOR, 1998

Bombay-born Anish Kapoor (*b.* 1954) is interested in the void, which he calls the "in-between space." His massive, mystical sculptures represent the void through forms with deep hollows. Looking up into *At the Edge of the World II* is a disorienting experience. It is impossible to tell where the cavity ends. By creating supreme emptiness, Kapoor offers a sense of infinity. When a viewer looks into one of Kapoor's empty blue half-spheres, the back is dark, invisible, and difficult to grasp. If the viewer makes a noise, however, the sculpture amplifies the sound to give a suggestion of the space.

HOUSE, *Rachel Whiteread, 1993*

*This huge, inverted sculpture of a house in Bow, London, by Rachel Whiteread* (right), *captured the memories and lives of the people who once lived there.*

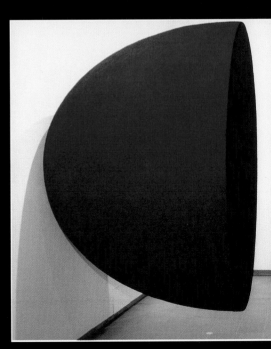

UNTITLED, *Anish Kapoor, 1990*

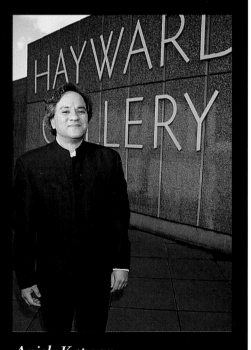

*Anish Kapoor*

## IS ANYTHING THERE?

Some of Kapoor's works are colored with a bright, powdery pigment. Others are cast in shiny, reflective metal or carved in stone. They all play with space, blurring the boundaries between visible and invisible. *When I Am Pregnant* (1992), for example, is a white bulge that juts out from the gallery wall but can be seen only from the side. When the viewer stands facing it straight on, the wall appears flat!

# ABSTRACT COLORS

Abstract art had its first wave of popularity between 1910 and 1920, and it has remained a key part of the art scene ever since. Instead of trying to depict subjects realistically, abstract art focuses on form and color.

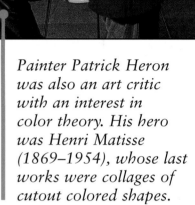

*Painter Patrick Heron was also an art critic with an interest in color theory. His hero was Henri Matisse (1869–1954), whose last works were collages of cutout colored shapes.*

## ABSTRACT LANDSCAPES

Even the most abstract art can still be inspired by nature. British artist Bridget Riley (*b.* 1931) produced large oil paintings of colored vertical stripes, such as *Burnished Sky* (1985), and diagonal paintings of distorted diamonds, such as *Certain Day* (1989). Each of these works has a grid behind it, but despite the mathematical precision, the paintings suggest landscapes — and not just because of their titles. Although known for black and white acrylics in the 1960s, Riley's palette changed in the 1980s. She now uses earthy oranges, pinks, and reds along with sky blues and grassy greens.

*Damien Hirst appeared with one of his "dot" paintings at the Turner Prize ceremony in 1995.*

### DOTTY DAMIEN
Best known for displaying sharks or cows in formaldehyde, Damien Hirst (*b.* 1965) also produces paintings. His two key styles of the 1990s were "spin" paintings, which were made by spinning paint onto the canvas, and "dot" paintings.

## TAKEN FROM NATURE

The Cornish landscape inspired the paintings of British artist Patrick Heron (1920–1999), but his work became increasingly abstract. It can be hard to recognize a rock or a tree among Heron's bold, scribbly shapes. Heron believed that all painting was abstract, yet it made "the outside world visible" — or, at least, the artist's view of it. Heron thought that beauty was found in a painting's rhythm, the way different parts of the painting relate to each other and lead the viewer's eye. He said, "The subject matter of a painting is the least important thing."

## ST. JOHN
### GERHARD RICHTER, 1988

*St. John* is one of Richter's "London Paintings," which were abstract works in oil inspired by trips to the chapels at Westminster Abbey in London. Many of Richter's works resemble the Impressionist paintings of French artist Claude Monet (1840–1926). As in Monet's famous "Water Lilies" series, Richter's colors merge and wobble like watery reflections. The works of both artists feature layers of thick color that make a built-up, textured surface. While Monet was trying to represent his impression of the landscape, however, Richter insists that he is not trying to show the external world at all. In *St. John*, Richter wanted to show how being in St. John's Chapel made him feel, rather than what St. John's Chapel looked like.

## COMMON INSPIRATION — MANY STYLES

Heron admired Henri Matisse (1869–1954), one of the first artists to explore abstraction. Matisse wanted to make restful works, "like a good armchair." Matisse also inspired David Hockney (*b.* 1937), whose abstract works feature bright, joyful shapes. Hockney does more than abstracts, however. His other styles include photomontage. German artist Gerhard Richter (*b.* 1932) also switches between *Abstraktes Bild,* or abstract painting, and photo-realistic painting.

*British artist David Hockney shot to fame in the 1960s with his Pop paintings of swimming pools and decadent living. His works in the 1990s included Matisse-inspired explorations of abstraction.*

# PAINT AND EMOTION

After the wide experimentation with art forms and the dominance of sculpture during the 1960s and 1970s, the 1980s brought a renewed interest in painting. In 1981, London's Royal Academy of Arts held an exhibition called "A New Spirit in Painting," which featured large, intense works from all over Europe.

## THE TRANSAVANTGARDE

In Italy, this emotional painting movement was called the Transavantgarde. Key artists were Sandro Chia (*b.* 1946), Mimmo Paladino (*b.* 1948), Enzo Cucchi (*b.* 1949), and Francesco Clemente (*b.* 1952). All four produced expressive figures, but each in a particular style. Chia fills every inch (centimeter) of the canvas with paint, while Cucchi's mystical works can be sparse. Clemente and Paladino produce dark, frightening pieces.

*As revelers pulled down the Berlin Wall, Germany became one country again.*

### THE WALL FALLS

German painters often used their art to work through their feelings about the country's recent history, especially the Nazi cruelties before and during World War II. When Germany was defeated in 1945, the country split into two separate states with the city of Berlin half East German and half West German, separated by the Berlin Wall until 1989.

*Sandro Chia is a prolific artist. He often paints his figures in heroic or classical poses, and his colorful style is not as gloomy as that of his contemporaries.*

## LILITH
### ANSELM KIEFER, 1987–1989

Lilith is a mythological figure. Babylonians knew her as Lilit, the evil ghost of desolate places. After a trip to Brazil, Kiefer portrayed the city of Sao Paulo as a desolate place. He mixed ash into the oil paint to show the filth and pollution produced by industry, and he added tangled wire at the bottom of the painting to show how scrambled the city's communication was.

## THE NEO-EXPRESSIONISTS

In Germany, the use of heavy blobs and smears of paint was the perfect way to express emotions about ongoing German history. German artists known as neo-Expressionists included Georg Baselitz (*b*. 1938) and A. R. Penck (*b*. 1939), both of whom can remember the bombing of Dresden. Baselitz's work is gloomy and unsettling. He often gives his people huge, blank eyes.

## DEATH AND DESTRUCTION

Other neo-Expressionists include Markus Lüpertz (*b*. 1941), Anselm Kiefer (*b*. 1945), and Rainer Fetting (*b*. 1949). Death and decay dominate Kiefer's paintings, which are often based on mythological stories. Kiefer is known to mix organic materials, such as straw, into his paint. These materials eventually decompose. Kiefer's canvases sometimes feature lead or copper, which also change over time as they corrode in the air.

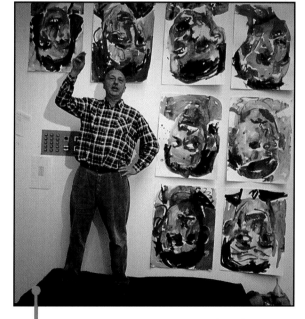

*Since 1969, Georg Baselitz has hung his blotchy paintings upside down. He actually paints them this way. This technique forces the viewer to experience the thickly painted surface of the piece, rather than concentrate just on the image.*

13

# BAD PAINTING

Neo-Expressionism also appeared in the United States. Its rough, crude style, which was used to symbolize the poverty of civilization as a whole, led to the term "Bad Painting." Some critics wrote off this new generation of art as too careless and raw. Others discovered that some Bad Painting was actually *good*!

*In the 1980s, British prime minister Margaret Thatcher shared U.S. president Reagan's economic ideas.*

### THE REAGAN YEARS

Ronald Reagan was president of the United States from 1981 to 1989. While in power, he cut taxes dramatically, promoting an economic boom. Until the stock market crash of 1987, wages increased and people had more to spend on luxury goods, including art.

## MATERIALS WITH MEANING

In the early 1980s, the brightest star on the U.S. art scene was Julian Schnabel (*b.* 1951). He skyrocketed to fame with his plate paintings, which were a kind of collage. The paintings featured pieces of clay or ceramic pottery with thick, gloppy paint under and over them. Schnabel left some plates whole but smashed others so their sharp edges stuck out of the picture. The broken pieces represented society's violence and aggression. Thick, dull-colored paint symbolized the excesses of greediness in the 1980s. "I wanted to make something that was exploding as much as I wanted to make something cohesive," Schnabel explained.

14

*The financial boom of the 1980s created millionaire art enthusiasts. Wall Street, New York's financial district, was at the heart of the boom. Wall Street is home to the New York and American stock exchanges and the Federal Reserve Bank.*

## MIXED MESSAGES

In his work, Schnabel recycles old styles of art that often conflict with each other. His subject matter ranges from Norse mythology to recent history, as though he is trying to show everything in the world in each picture. Schnabel's work is also deeply personal. It is his way of making an impression on a fragmented world. "I want my life to be embedded in my work," he said, ". . . crushed into my painting, like a pressed car."

# HUMANITY ASLEEP

## Julian Schnabel, 1982

*Humanity Asleep* is one of Schnabel's pottery-embedded plate paintings. Thick, crudely applied paint gives the piece a raised surface, or relief effect. It looks rough, almost like it was painted by a child. Although this painting was done on canvas, Schnabel worked on a variety of surfaces, including carpeting and velvet.

*Trump Tower, part of the real estate empire of multimillionaire Donald Trump, opened in 1983. Many high-living New Yorkers rented apartments there, including gallery owner Jeffrey Deitch, who made a fortune during the art boom of the 1980s.*

## WHOSE ART?

For one of his pieces, Schnabel bought a diptych called *Daemonization* (1980) by fellow-American and "Bad" painter David Salle (*b.* 1952). Schnabel switched the two panels of the diptych around and painted a portrait of Salle on top of one of them. He titled the painting *Jump* (1980) and signed it as his own, raising questions about who the artist of the piece was and what the piece meant. Both Schnabel and Salle used their work to turn traditional ideas about art upside down.

*In his paintings of the early 1980s, Schnabel used a variety of cheap pottery — some plain and some patterned. He stuck the pieces on with cement or industrial adhesives. Schnabel's finished paintings sold for astronomical amounts of money.*

# GRAFFITI ART

New York was the capital of the art world throughout the 1980s. The most exclusively American movement at the time was Graffiti Art, which had its roots in the artistic vandalism found on New York subways. Key figures of this movement were Jean-Michel Basquiat (1960–1988) and Keith Haring (1958–1990).

*Basquiat was a snappy dresser. He even wore expensive Armani suits while painting.*

## ARROZ CON POLLO (RICE AND CHICKEN)
### JEAN-MICHEL BASQUIAT, 1981

Although Basquiat's work first appeared on walls and often featured scrawled writing or symbols, he claimed, "My work has nothing to do with graffiti. It is painting and it always has been." Basquiat drew on African, Puerto Rican, and Haitian imagery, such as fetishes, crucifixes, skulls, and totems. In *Arroz con Pollo,* named after a Carribean dish, the figure on the left looks like a devil or a voodoo doll stuck with pins.

*Drug abuse was an increasing problem during the 1980s. The message of many of Keith Haring's New York murals, or wall paintings, such as* Crack is Wack *(1987), was that taking drugs is bad.*

## CARTOONS WITH A MESSAGE

Haring's cartoonlike art, with its thick black outlines and stylized figures, is instantly recognizable. It was popular on greetings cards and T-shirts, but it was also put to serious use. In *Ignorance=Fear* (1989), for example, Haring reinterpreted the three monkeys (See No Evil, Hear No Evil, and Speak No Evil) for an AIDS awareness poster.

## IN THE END

Both Haring and Basquiat died tragically young — Haring of AIDS and Basquiat of a drug overdose. After Basquiat's death, painter Julian Schnabel made a film about his life.

### AIDS AWARENESS

Acquired Immune Deficiency Syndrome, or AIDS, is a terrible disease that destroys the body's natural defenses. HIV, the virus that causes AIDS, was identified in 1983. Since then, charity groups, such as ACT UP in the United States and the Terence Higgins Trust in Britain, have worked hard to fight this illness by raising public awareness.

*British artists Gilbert & George appeared with their picture* Bleeding *at an AIDS charity event in May 1989.*

# BIG SCULPTURES

Large-scale sculptures that had become popular during the 1960s and 1970s continued to appear in the 1980s and 1990s. Many of them were new works by established artists of the earlier decades.

## OLD STYLES REVISITED

In New York, Pop artist Roy Lichtenstein (1923–1997) carried on his cartoonlike style with large, painted metal sculptures of three-dimensional brushstrokes, such as *Mural with Blue Brushstrokes* (1986). Claes Oldenburg (*b.* 1929) and Coosje van Bruggen (*b.* 1942) also created gigantic Pop sculptures, such as their oversized needle and thread (2000) in Milan, Italy. Christo (*b.* 1935) and Jeanne-Claude (*b.* 1935) continued their environmental work. Their wrapping of entire buildings included the German parliament, the Reichstag, in 1995.

*In Rebecca Horn's Concert for Anarchy, the burst-open piano represents traditional, male culture turned, literally, upside down.*

18

### MICRO SCULPTURES

At the same time artists were creating large-scale sculptures, Willard Wigan started making record-breakingly tiny ones!

BOXING RING, *Willard Wigan*

## MELANCHOLY MACHINES

Large-scale works tend to take things out of context, forcing the viewer to look at them with new eyes. For this reason, they often bring about uneasiness or a sense of dislocation. German artist Rebecca Horn (*b.* 1944) is known for her disturbing mechanical sculptures. Her *Concert for Anarchy* (1990), for example, features a bursting grand piano hanging upside down over the viewer's head. This work suggests the idea of hanging on to sanity by a thread, threatening destruction if it snaps. Horn says, "The tragic and melancholic aspect of machines is very important to me."

## FORMIDABLE FEMALES

Other artistic women whose work explored ideas of female creativity included Louise Bourgeois (*b.* 1911) and Yayoi Kusama (*b.* 1929) in America and Helen Chadwick (1953–1996) and Tracey Emin (*b.* 1963) in Britain.

*This huge, three-dimensional, inflatable sculpture by Japanese-born Yayoi Kusama has Pop-Art styling.*

## MAMAN
### LOUISE BOURGEOIS, 1999

The works of French-born sculptor Louise Bourgeois are often autobiographical. *Maman*, for example, expresses her ideas about motherhood. (*Maman* is French for "mommy.") Bourgeois created *Maman* for the Tate Modern gallery in London. At 30 feet (9 meters) high, *Maman* is the largest in a series of spider sculptures by Bourgeois. It is made of steel and has white marble eggs under its body. Because of the beautiful but deadly web it weaves, the spider symbolizes femininity, entrapment, and artistic creation.

# BOLD MATERIALS

The desire to shock or provoke has led many artists to experiment with new and unusual media and materials.

## ANIMAL MAGIC

Damien Hirst uses a wide variety of materials. His works include wall displays that feature collections of objects, such as seashells or surgical instruments. He is best known, however, for his vitrines, or glass tanks, containing animals or fish preserved in formaldehyde. *Mother and Child Divided* (1993) is a vitrine with a cow and a calf cut in two.

*Besides using elephant dung in his artwork, Chris Ofili makes stands out of it to display his finished pieces.*

## ANIMAL MATTER

British artist Chris Ofili (*b.* 1968) is known for creating decorative works in lush colors, and he often makes collages using magazine clippings, sequins, human hair, and even elephant dung. Thinking he might be pigeonholed as a black artist, Ofili did not want his blackness to be treated as exotic and ethnic. The elephant dung is meant to show that not everything from Africa is exotic! Ofili explains, "I made a decision to make these paintings that were really ornate and . . . I wanted to include something in the paintings that would criticize that — to challenge that."

### THE PHYSICAL IMPOSSIBILITY OF DEATH IN THE MIND OF SOMEONE LIVING
#### DAMIEN HIRST, 1991

Hirst's most notorious vitrine display features a dead tiger shark. Most people refer to the work as *Shark*, but its true title is a clue to what the piece really means — that all living things ultimately die. This piece also comments on how living things are displayed in museums, where they become lifeless objects taken out of their natural environments. Finally, this vitrine offers the fascinating experience of being able to see a scary shark close up — but as an object of beauty rather than a figure of fear.

*Damien Hirst is the best-known British artist of his generation.*

## OFILI IN AFRICA

Chris Ofili was born in Manchester, England, but his parents were originally from Nigeria, West Africa. Ofili's own African experience came with a scholarship to Zimbabwe in 1992. In Zimbabwe, he came across some ancient dot paintings on cave walls. The paintings were made by the Matopos people, and their decorative style inspired Ofili's work. Ofili was also fascinated with body scarring, which is a religious practice of the Nuba people in Sudan, East Africa. Decorating the body this way often marks an important event in a person's life, such as coming of age.

*Body scarring is both a religious ritual and an art form.*

## THE ULTIMATE BODY ART

Another British artist, Marc Quinn (*b.* 1964), rose to fame with a unique self-portrait simply called *Self* (1991). This sculpture must be kept refrigerated. It is the artist's own head cast in his own frozen blood. Quinn's work was a continuation of Body Art, which became popular in the 1960s.

# KITSCH IS COOL

Reacting against the supercharged emotion of the Abstract Expressionists, Pop artists of the 1960s took their shallow subject matter from popular culture. In the 1980s, a new generation of artists was inspired by tacky goods. Was their art cynical and empty, or was it a cool comment on greed and capitalism?

### KITSCH CULTURE
Jean-Paul Gaultier, the fashion designer who put men in skirts and popularized underwear as outer wear, also co-presented *Eurotrash*, a TV show of Kitsch clips from across Europe. French artists Pierre et Gilles photographed Gaultier in a sentimental setting, surrounded by daisies (*Jean Paul*, 1990).

22

*Jean-Paul Gaultier proudly displays his own kind of kitsch.*

## STOCK SCHLOCK
The new style was called Kitsch or Schlock, meaning trashy, sugary, and sentimental. It typically included cute little animals, flowers, or religious icons. The French art team Pierre et Gilles (*f.* 1977) photographed famous stars, such as Boy George, Paloma Picasso, and Catherine Deneuve, looking like Christian saints, figures from Greek myths, or Hindu gods.

*At first, Kitsch copied tacky items sold in gift shops. Later, gift shops were inspired by Kitsch! There was a market for items that were deliberately in bad taste, such as this glow-in-the-dark St. Clare.*

## KITSCH KOONS
The most successful Kitsch artist, Jeff Koons (*b.* 1955), started out putting ordinary objects, such as vacuum cleaners or basketballs, in plastic cases like museum displays. Then, he made replicas of tasteless souvenirs.

## PRETTY PUPPY
Since 1997, Koons's *Puppy* has guarded the front door of the Guggenheim Museum in Bilbao, Spain. This West Highland terrier is 43 feet (13 m) tall and is made from more than seventy thousand flowering plants. It was inspired by a pottery pup Koons saw in a gift shop.

## POPPLES
### JEFF KOONS, 1988

*Popples* is part of Koons's fourth series of work, known as "Statuary." The sculptures in this series are all porcelain copies of soft toys. Other Statuary pieces include *Amore* (1988), a cute bear in a bib and diaper. Koons, who used to be a Wall Street broker, makes seemingly meaningless objects monumental. He forces viewers to look closely at trivial, sentimental objects and think about ideas of beauty and taste. The overwhelming sense is that the objects are being celebrated and enjoyed for what they are. The fun Koons creates is most evident in *Balloon Dog* (1995), a shiny metal sculpture that looks exactly like the balloon animals entertainers make at children's birthday parties.

*Like Pop artist Andy Warhol, Jeff Koons does not make his pieces himself. His role as an artist is choosing the objects and deciding how they will look.*

23

# CAUGHT ON CAMERA

Since the 19th century, many people have considered photography to be art's poor cousin. With more and more artists pushing photography to the limit, however, critics have been forced to recognize the creativity and control demanded by the camera.

## THE CAMERA NEVER LIES?

Some artists use the camera to create scenes that are far from real. American Cindy Sherman (*b.* 1954) has done a series of photographic self-portraits in which she appears as movie stars or historical figures. In *Untitled #193* (1991), for example, she is an 18th-century French lady with a powdered wig! Other artists create fantasy realms with computer-manipulated photographs. Japanese video and performance artist Mariko Mori (*b.* 1967) appears in stunning sci-fi settings.

24

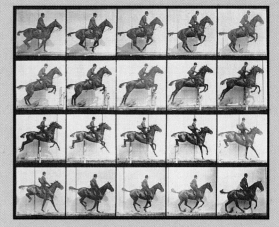

MAN AND HORSE JUMPING A FENCE, *Eadweard Muybridge,* 1887

### MOVING PICTURES

English photographer Eadweard Muybridge (1830–1904) was one of the first to see the possibilities of photography. He published his eleven-volume *Animal Locomotion* in 1887. Muybridge set his studies of the bodies of people and animals in motion with a row of cameras that clicked off shots one by one, using as many as twenty-four cameras for one sequence.

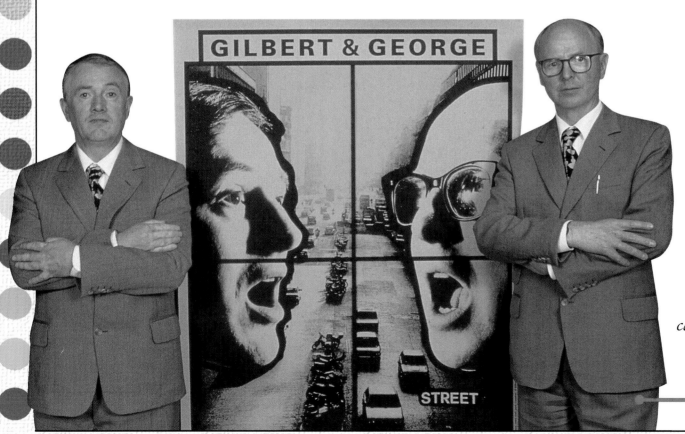

*Gilbert Proesch (b. 1943) (left) and George Passmore (b. 1942) (right) became the single artist "Gilbert & George" in 1967. Using photographs of men — usually themselves — they create huge works with bright, gaudy tints. Although the pieces are flat and two-dimensional, Gilbert & George call them sculptures.*

STREET, *Gilbert & George, c. 1983*

## ABSTRACT ART

German artist Andreas Gursky (*b*. 1955) has used a computer to clean up his photographs since 1992, but his images depend primarily on the strength of his compositions. Typically, Gursky chooses a landscape or a cityscape with small, repeated elements, so it looks almost abstract. "My preference for clear structures," he says, "is the result of my desire . . . to keep track of things and maintain my grip on the world." He chooses a semi-aerial view so any people, such as the workers in *Stock Exchange, Tokyo* (1990) or the people in *Hong Kong, Grand Hyatt Park* (1994), are reduced to antlike figures.

PEARBLOSSOM HIGHWAY 11–18TH APRIL 1986 #2, *David Hockney, 1986*

*British artist David Hockney used hundreds of different photographs to create a landscape. He began making his photographic "patchworks" in the 1980s.*

## PARIS, MONTPARNASSE
### ANDREAS GURSKY, 1993

This panorama is huge — more than 10 feet (3 m) wide — and shows endless rows of tiny windows on tower blocks along a Parisian street, Montparnasse. The repetition suggests a common Gursky theme that life in an urban environment is compartmentalized.

Gursky prefers a horizontal format for his works so the viewer's eye darts back and forth across the flat surface, making connections. In the end, the main feature is the sense of a universal order — the pattern that unifies all of the tiny, individual elements.

# VIDEO ART

Throughout the 20th century, artists worked with existing media, such as painting and sculpture. When video exploded on the scene, however, a whole new medium was born.

### VERSATILE VIDEO

Video can record performance art, tell a story, or display abstract images. It can be viewed in a darkened room inside a gallery or projected onto huge public billboards. Video art can be shown on a single screen, as in *I Do Not Know What It Is I Am Like* (1986) by Bill Viola, a film of the artist reflected in an owl's eye. It can also be displayed on many screens at once, as in *Rio Videowall* (1989) by Dara Birnbaum (*b*. 1946). Video walls allow the artist to explore relationships between parts of the image, or to compare different images.

## HIGH TECH ALLERGY
(DETAIL)
NAM JUNE PAIK, 1996

Korean-born Nam June Paik (*b*. 1932) is the father of Video Art. His footage of the Pope's visit to the United States in 1965 was the first video piece ever made. *High Tech Allergy* is one of a family of robots Paik built out of televisions. Paik started out in the 1960s as a performance artist with the experimental Fluxus group. Today, Paik's robots are performers in their own right!

Electronic Superhighway, *Paik's entry for the 1993 Venice Bienniale, was made of hundreds of television sets placed among lush, tropical plants and objects from popular culture — including cars.*

### VIDEO SURVEILLANCE

Many video artists explore how television controls people's lives. For *HIDEO, It's Me, Mama* (1983), Japanese artist Mako Idemitsu (*b*. 1940) created the fictional character Hideo, whose life unfolds, via video, on television. The same idea was behind the Hollywood movie *The Truman Show* (1998). Truman is a happy enough fellow, until he finds out that everyone around him, including his wife, is an actor, and that his life is the plot of an all-day soap opera watched by millions.

*Actor Jim Carrey has the lead role in* The Truman Show *(1998).*

**ELECTRONIC SUPERHIGHWAY:
BILL CLINTON STOLE MY IDEA** (DETAIL)
NAM JUNE PAIK, 1993

*The video work of British artist Steve McQueen (b. 1969) reacts against the Hollywood stereotypes of black men. Bear (1993) shows McQueen in a boxing match. In Deadpan (1997), he reenacts a scene from an old silent movie, with himself in the starring role.*

## CHANNEL DISTURBANCE

Multiple-channel works give artists a chance to put unlikely images next to each other. On one screen of the diptych *Ever Is Over All* (1997), by Swiss artist Pipilotti Rist (*b.* 1962), a smiling woman walks along the street humming but, every so often, stops to smash car windows with a red-hot metal poker shaped like a flower. In contrast, the second screen shows real flowers. The overall effect is disturbing, if not violent. Twins Jane and Louise Wilson (*b.* 1967) also create distressing video art. They shoot films in locations that produce resonant sound. *Stasi City* (1997) is set in the abandoned headquarters of the East German secret police. *Gamma (Silo)* (1999) is in an old nuclear weapons base at Greenham Common, England.

# COMPUTER-AGE ART

The very first digital pictures were made in the 1960s — by scientists! They were the only people with access to computers and the only ones who could master the long strings of complex commands to operate them. During the 1980s, computers became easier to use and more affordable.

## MACHINE-MADE

From early on, people have used computers to generate geometric patterns, but today, the artistic opportunities are endless. Not only is it possible to manipulate paintings and photos, but, with innovative software, artists also can make three-dimensional objects that exist only on-screen.

## BUILDING NEW WORLDS

British artist William Latham (*b.* 1961) was one of the first to create virtual organisms (*www.artworks.co.uk*). In *The Evolution of Form* (1990), beautifully patterned three-dimensional creatures mutate and evolve. With works such as *Galápagos* (1997), American artist Karl Sims (*b.* 1962) (*www.genarts.com/karl*) also explores evolution. His art is interactive, so the viewer can choose environments for the organisms.

## MEANWHILE, BACK IN THE (REAL) WORLD . . .

Digital art has had a far-reaching influence even on artists who do not produce it. Thanks to the Internet, artists no longer have to rely on exhibitions to show their work to the public. Many, including Claes Oldenburg, have home pages that act as permanent galleries.

28

## THE COOKER
### JAKE TILSON, 1994 and onward
### www.thecooker.com

British artist Jake Tilson (*b.* 1958) is one of many web artists who display their work on-line. The Internet allows artists to create multilayered work that mixes images, text, animation, and sound. The work is often open-ended. Because viewers can move around the site by choosing their own links, artists have no control over the order in which images or words are seen. Tilson believes, "You have to allow uncertainty into art. It's that little seep of chaos that creeps in — you have to be ready for it, react to it, and let it sit there." At the beginning of the 20th century, the artist was seen as the controller who presented a completed image to the viewer. Web art lets the viewer finish the piece. Other than its ability to reach such an enormous audience, this aspect of web art is one of the most revolutionary.

*Completed in 1946, ENIAC, one of the very first computers, was as big as a room! Portable laptop computers were developed by the 1980s.*

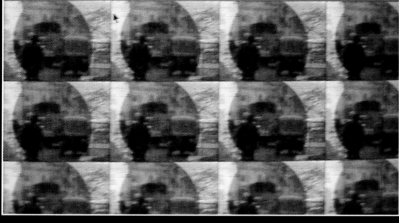

*Museum of Modern Art: www.moma.org*

*The Guggenheim: www.guggenheim.org*

*The Tate: www.tate.org.uk*

*Major art institutions, such as those listed above, developed their own web sites during the 1980s and 1990s. Visit these sites or search the web to find others. Most sites let you view their art collections on-line.*

## C.G. CINEMA

Computers have revolutionized many art forms. *Toy Story* (1995) was the first full-length computer-generated (C.G.) movie. This instant classic is a tale of rivalry between two toys, but the main attraction was the medium, not the message. Eighty-one minutes of film took the equivalent of forty-six continuous days of computer processing.

*Buzz Lightyear and Woody are* Toy Story's *digital stars.*